Russian Blue Cats

Stephanie Finne

Checkerboard
Library

An Imprint of Abdo Publishing
www.abdopublishing.com

www.abdopublishing.com

Published by Abdo Publishing, a division of ABDO, PO Box 398166, Minneapolis, MN 55439.
Copyright © 2015 by Abdo Consulting Group, Inc. International copyrights reserved in all
countries. No part of this book may be reproduced in any form without written permission from
the publisher. Checkerboard Library™ is a trademark and logo of Abdo Publishing.

Printed in the United States of America, North Mankato, Minnesota.
032014
092014

Cover Photo: Photo by Helmi Flick
Interior Photos: Alamy p. 15; Glow Images pp. 7, 19; Photo by Helmi Flick p. 13;
    iStockphoto pp. 1, 5, 9, 11, 21; Thinkstock pp. 16–17

Series Coordinator: Bridget O'Brien
Editors: Tamara L. Britton, Megan M. Gunderson
Art Direction: Renée LaViolette

Library of Congress Cataloging-in-Publication Data

Finne, Stephanie.
  Russian Blue cats / Stephanie Finne.
      pages. cm. -- (Cats)
  Includes index.
  Audience: Age 8-12.
  ISBN 978-1-62403-326-1
  1. Russian Blue cat--Juvenile literature. I. Title.
  SF449.R86F56 2014
  636.8'2--dc23
                    2013048629

Contents

Lions, Tigers, and Cats

Wild cats have been on Earth for thousands of years. About 3,500 years ago, ancient Egyptians began taming cats. These cats hunted **rodents** and kept pests away from grains and crops. Today's **domestic** cats are descendants of these early cats.

Today, there are 37 cat species. All these cats belong to the family **Felidae**, including the Russian blue cat. They are one of 40 different domestic **breeds**.

Russian blue cats are often compared to their wild cousins. This breed has sharp senses. They are also **cautious** and take time to watch strangers. But unlike wild cats, Russian blues make great family companions.

Russian blues are loving pets. They are very attached to their owners.

Russian Blue Cats

The Russian blue is a natural **breed**. It is believed that these cats began in Russia's Archangel Isles. This has led to them being called Archangel cats.

Knowledge of the Russian blue's beginnings is lost to history. However, some legends say Russian blues may have been hunted for their unusual fur. Others claim Russian blues were favorite cats of kings. **Folktales** say these cats had healing powers and could also bring good luck!

By the mid-1800s, Russian blue cats had been brought to the rest of Europe. Russian blues competed in early cat shows there. In the early 1900s, Russian blues came to the United States. In 1949, they were accepted for registration by the **Cat Fanciers' Association**.

During the 1960s, breeders began to selectively breed Russian blues to produce kittens with silver coats and

green eyes. Soon, the **breed** became more popular. Today, Russian blues are favorite show cats and loving family companions.

Over time, Russian blues have had many names. Some of these are foreign blue, Spanish blue, and Russian shorthair.

Qualities

Russian blues are **cautious** cats. They take time to observe what is happening before entering a situation. Because they are shy, people think blues are not friendly. But once they decide you are worthy, blues are wonderful companions.

Blues love being with their family. They will follow their humans from room to room. They can sense what is going on around them. They will clown around to lighten the mood. If they sense a person does not like cats, they will do everything they can to change that person's mind!

Once Russian blues are comfortable in their home, they are playful. They love to play fetch and are great jumpers.

Blues are also smart. They will remember where you put their favorite feather or their food. They can learn how to open drawers to get to hidden things!

Coat and Color

The Russian blue cat has a very **dense** coat. The double coat is water resistant. It is almost like the fur of a seal or a beaver. It protected the cat from harsh Russian winters.

This **breed** has only one coat color, blue. The coat's blue **guard hairs** are tipped in silver. This makes the Russian blue look like it is frosted with powdered sugar. The cat shimmers as it moves!

The **plush**, silky coat looks beautiful with the Russian blue's eyes. The breed's large, round eyes come in only one color, a striking green. The emerald eyes are the color of the Russian forest.

It may take a while to see those green eyes! The shy Russian blue doesn't like to look people in the eye.

Size

Russian blue cats are medium-sized cats. Their bodies are long and muscular. Female Russian blues weigh between five and eight pounds (2.2 and 3.6 kg). Males are larger at seven to ten pounds (3.1 to 4.5 kg).

The head of the Russian blue is a medium wedge shape. It features a smooth **muzzle** and a slate gray nose. The ears are large and have pointed tips.

The fine-boned Russian blue has long legs. They end in slightly rounded paws. The blue has five toes on the front paws and four toes on the hind paws. The graceful Russian blue looks as if it is dancing on tiptoes.

A blue's curved mouth makes the cat appear to be smiling!

Care

Russian blue cats need regular health care. A veterinarian will examine your pet and give it required **vaccines**. He or she will also **spay** or **neuter** your cat.

Like its wild relatives, your Russian blue will need to bury its waste. So, you will need a **litter box**. Make sure to clean it out every day. Wild cats sharpen their claws on trees. Provide a scratching post to avoid damage to your couch! Russian blues also enjoy perching in high places and watching out windows.

Russian blues are clean cats that need little grooming. General grooming includes cleaning their ears, trimming their claws, and brushing their fur.

The most important part of caring for your Russian blue cat is having patience. This **breed** likes to take things slowly. Introduce them to your home one room at a time. It is best to select one room for the first few days or weeks. Then slowly add new rooms. Once Russian blues are comfortable, you will be surprised where you find them!

Russian blues are good at hide-and-seek. They like to hide in small spaces.

Feeding

All cats need a balanced diet that includes meat. There are different types of cat food. These include dry, semimoist, and canned foods. Choose one that is labeled "complete and balanced." This food contains all the **nutrients** your cat needs.

Feeding your cat can be done in one of three ways. Food can be measured out, or portion fed. It can be fed at specific times of day, or time fed. Or, food can always be available. This is called free fed.

You can discuss feeding options with your vet. No matter how you choose to feed your cat, it is important that it always has fresh water.

Russian blues love food! They can overeat, so watch how much food you provide. Indoor cats can easily become overweight. This can lead to health problems.

17

Most cats like
to eat from
shallow bowls.

Kittens

Russian blue cats are wonderful mothers. Like other cats, they are able to mate when they are 7 to 12 months old. After mating, female cats are **pregnant** for about 65 days. When a cat gives birth, it is called kittening.

Kittens are born blind, deaf, and helpless. Russian blue kittens weigh just two to three ounces (57 to 85 g) at birth. After 10 to 12 days, they can see and hear. Their teeth begin to grow in. When they are three weeks old, they begin to explore their world.

For the first five weeks, kittens drink their mother's milk. Then, they are **weaned** onto solid food. The kittens spend their days learning and growing. They are able to leave their mother at 12 to 16 weeks old.

Russian blue cats are born with blue eyes. The color then changes to khaki or gold. By four months old, the eyes should have some green in them. The eyes will be their final green color when the kittens are a year old.

Russian blue mothers usually have three kittens in a litter. But sometimes there can be more!

Buying a Kitten

Have you decided the Russian blue is the right cat for your family? If so, find a good **breeder**. Good breeders sell healthy cats that have had **vaccinations**. They also know the history of their cats. They will be able to suggest a kitten that is the right fit for your family.

If you are thinking about getting a Russian blue, be sure to visit it first. It is a good idea to visit it more than once. Each time, wait 24 hours to see if any allergic reactions appear. If no allergies appear, you are all set to get a Russian blue.

Before bringing home your cat, be sure to have needed supplies ready. Food and water dishes, food, and a **litter box** will be needed right away. You are now ready for your new best friend! With attention, annual health care, and good food, your Russian blue will be a loving member of your family for 10 to 15 years.

Russian blues are one of the least destructive cat breeds. They make wonderful indoor pets!

Glossary

breed - a group of animals sharing the same ancestors and appearance. A breeder is a person who raises animals. Raising animals is often called breeding them.

Cat Fanciers' Association - a group that sets the standards for judging all breeds of cats.

cautious - taking special care to avoid problems or danger.

dense - thick or compact.

domestic - tame, especially relating to animals.

Felidae (FEHL-uh-dee) - the scientific Latin name for the cat family. Members of this family are called felids. They include lions, tigers, leopards, jaguars, cougars, wildcats, lynx, cheetahs, and domestic cats.

folktale - a story handed down from person to person. A folktale is not usually set in a particular time or place.

guard hair - one of the long, coarse hairs that protects a mammal's undercoat.

litter box - a box filled with cat litter, which is similar to sand. Cats use litter boxes to bury their waste.

muzzle - an animal's nose and jaws.

neuter (NOO-tuhr) - to remove a male animal's reproductive glands.

nutrient - a substance found in food and used in the body. It promotes growth, maintenance, and repair.

plush - thick and soft.

pregnant - having one or more babies growing within the body.

rodent - any of several related animals that have large front teeth for gnawing. Common rodents include mice, squirrels, and beavers.

spay - to remove a female animal's reproductive organs.

vaccine (vak-SEEN) - a shot given to prevent illness or disease.

wean - to accustom an animal to eating food other than its mother's milk.

Websites

To learn more about Cats,
visit **booklinks.abdopublishing.com**. These links are routinely
monitored and updated to provide the most current information available.

Index